ON
THE HERO'S
JOURNEY

JOSEPH CAMPBELL ESSENTIALS

ON THE HERO'S JOURNEY

JOSEPH CAMPBELL

JOSEPH CAMPBELL™
FOUNDATION

NEW WORLD LIBRARY

New World Library
Novato, California

New World Library
14 Pamaron Way
Novato, California 94949

Text design by Tona Pearce Myers

Library of Congress Cataloging-in-Publication data is available.

First printing, September 2025
ISBN 978-1-955831-11-6
Printed in Canada

10   9   8   7   6   5   4   3   2   1

New World Library is committed to protecting our natural
environment. This book is made of material from well-
managed FSC®-certified forests and other controlled sources.

THE HERO is symbolical of that divine creative and redemptive image which is hidden within us all, only waiting to be known and rendered into life.

THAT'S THE BASIC motif of the universal hero's journey—leaving one condition and finding the source of life to bring you forth into a richer or mature condition.

THERE'S A CERTAIN type of myth which one might call the vision quest, going in quest of a boon, a vision, which has the same form in every mythology. That is the thing that I tried to present in the first book I wrote, *The Hero with a Thousand Faces*. All these different mythologies give us the same essential quest. You leave the world that you're in and go into a depth or into a distance or up to a height. There you come to what was missing in your consciousness in the world you formerly inhabited. Then comes the problem either of staying with that, and letting the world drop off, or returning with that boon and trying to hold on to it as you move back into your social world again. That's not an easy thing to do.

A PERSON is a hero or a heroine when he or she is functioning in the interest of values that are not local to the person but are of some greater force of which the person is a vehicle. The woman becomes a heroine as she becomes a vehicle of a force that brings forth life.

THE MYTHOLOGICAL hero, setting forth from his common-day hut or castle, is lured, carried away, or else voluntarily proceeds, to the threshold of adventure. There he encounters a shadow presence that guards the passage. The hero may defeat or conciliate this power and go alive into the kingdom of the dark (brother-battle, dragon-battle; offering, charm), or be slain by the opponent and descend in death (dismemberment, crucifixion). Beyond the threshold, then, the hero journeys through a world of unfamiliar yet strangely intimate forces, some of which severely threaten him (tests), some of which give magical aid (helpers). When he arrives at the nadir of the mythological round, he undergoes a supreme ordeal and gains his reward. The triumph may be represented as the hero's sexual union with the goddess-mother of the world (sacred marriage), his recognition by the father-creator (father atonement), his own divinization (apotheosis), or again—if the powers have remained unfriendly to him—his theft of the boon he came to gain (bride-theft, fire-theft); intrinsically it is an expansion of consciousness and therewith of being (illumination, transfiguration, freedom). The final work is that of the return. If the powers have blessed the hero, he now sets forth under their protection (emissary); if not, he flees and is pursued (transformation flight, obstacle flight). At the return threshold the transcendental powers must remain behind; the hero re-emerges from the kingdom of dread (return, resurrection). The boon that he brings restores the world (elixir).

IT'S A CYCLE of departure, tests, and ordeals, with a realization of some kind. It may be great. It may be little. But it gives you the sense of realization. And then the return with your realization to the society that you left, and somehow contributing to it what you've gained (bringing back the elixir, the boon). All the stories of founders of cities, founders of civilizations, founders of religions, founders of great art traditions, and so forth—that's the story. You'll find it one way or another. Those are the stages.

THE IDEA in the hero adventure is to walk bodily through the door into the world where the dualistic rules don't apply.

THE TWO WORLDS, the divine and the human, can be pictured only as distinct from each other—different as life and death, as day and night. The hero adventures out of the land we know into darkness; there accomplishes his adventure, or again is simply lost to us, imprisoned, or in danger; and his return is described as a coming back out of that yonder zone. Nevertheless—and here is a great key to the understanding of myth and symbol—the two kingdoms are actually one.

THE HERO JOURNEY through the threshold is simply a journey beyond the pairs of opposites, where you go beyond good and evil.

THE BUDDHA went into solitude and then sat beneath the bo tree, the tree of immortal knowledge, where he received an illumination that has enlightened all of Asia for twenty-five hundred years. After baptism by John the Baptist, Jesus went into the desert for forty days; and it was out of that desert that he came with his message. Moses went to the top of a mountain and came down with the tables of the law. Then you have the one who founds a new city—almost all the old Greek cities were founded by heroes who went off on quests and had surprising adventures, out of which each then founded a city. You might also say that the founder of a life—your life or mine, if we live our own lives, instead of imitating everybody else's life—comes from a quest as well.

ANOTHER CHALLENGE at the threshold can be the encounter with the dark counterpart, the shadow, where the shining hero meets the dark. It may be in the form of a dragon, or it may be in the form of a malignant enemy. In either case, the hero has to slay the other and go into the other world alive.

THERE ARE two types of deed. One is the physical deed, in which the hero performs a courageous act in battle or saves a life. The other kind is the spiritual deed, in which the hero learns to experience the supernormal range of human spiritual life and then comes back with a message. The usual hero adventure begins with someone from whom something has been taken, or who feels there's something lacking in the normal experiences available or permitted to the members of his society. This person then takes off on a series of adventures beyond the ordinary, either to recover what has been lost or to discover some life-giving elixir. It's usually a cycle, a going and a returning.

ONCE HAVING traversed the threshold, the hero moves in a dream landscape of curiously fluid, ambiguous forms, where he must survive a succession of trials. This is a favorite phase of the myth-adventure. It has produced a world literature of miraculous tests and ordeals. The hero is covertly aided by the advice, amulets, and secret agents of the supernatural helper whom he met before his entrance into this region. Or it may be that he here discovers for the first time that there is a benign power everywhere supporting him in his superhuman passage.

MYTHS COME OUT of the creative imagination we all share, and the story each of us recognizes in our own search for spiritual meaning parallels all the legends of heroes, like the knights of the Round Table, who must travel to an unknown world and do battle with the powers of darkness in order to return with the gift of knowledge.

A GOOD LIFE is one hero journey after another. Over and over again, you are called to the realm of adventure, you are called to new horizons. Each time, there is the same problem: Do I dare? And then if you do dare, the dangers are there, and the help also, and the fulfillment or the fiasco. There's always the possibility of a fiasco. But there's also the possibility of bliss.

WITH THE personifications of his destiny to guide and aid him, the hero goes forward in his adventure until he comes to the "threshold guardian" at the entrance to the zone of magnified power. Such custodians bound the world in the four directions—also up and down—standing for the limits of the hero's present sphere, or life horizon. Beyond them is darkness, the unknown, and danger; just as beyond the parental watch is danger to the infant and beyond the protection of his society danger to the member of the tribe.

THE FIRST FIGURE to come into collision with the individual is the shadow figure, those aspects of your own masculinity or femininity, your own actuality, that you have not assimilated. This must be assimilated. So stage one is the assimilation of the rejected elements [or] aspects of one's own character. Jung calls this swallowing the frog. This is going through the narrow pass.... The hero comes to the threshold of adventure and meets the dark one who is simply the other lost aspect of himself.

ONE IS BORN into a society. The society impresses on one certain ideals, certain aims, certain possibilities of life. These may not accord with one's own personal potentials. Or one may also, through one's intellect, see their defects and deficiencies. This is what happens with the dropout; it's a typical youthful experience: that those motifs that are being impressed on me for life do not correspond with those that are asking to come through. Then comes the business of questing. And you're going into a dark forest where no one has been before because you're looking for your own spiritual life, not that of somebody else. This leads you into realms of terrific danger. And there are typical crises. That first one, of moving away, is the one I term the Call to Adventure.

THE MORAL OBJECTIVE is that of saving a people, or saving a person, or supporting an idea. The hero sacrifices himself for something—that's the morality of it. Now, from another position, of course, you might say that the idea for which he sacrificed himself was something that should not have been respected. That's a judgment from the other side, but it doesn't destroy the intrinsic heroism of the deed performed.

THE SYMBOL of the crucified hero-figure . . . is a motif that occurs in many, many religious traditions. We find it among the Pawnee Indians, we find it among the Aztecs, we find it among the Mayans, we find it in the Prometheus figure, chained to the rock: the figure of the hero who, out of love, has brought the boon—the boon of atonement or the boon of fire or whatever it is—and for this purpose has given his own life, thoughtless of his own self.

THE HOLY GRAIL, hovering in air but covered with samite cloth, had appeared before the assembled knights in the dining hall of King Arthur and then, again, disappeared. Whereupon Arthur's nephew, Gawain, arose and proposed to all a vow, namely, to depart next day on a general quest, to behold the Grail unveiled. And indeed, next morning they departed. But here, then, comes the line. "They thought it would be a disgrace," we read, "to ride forth in a group. But each entered the forest at one point or another, there where he saw it to be thickest and there was no way or path." For where you are following a way or path, you

are following the way or destiny of
another. Your own, which is as yet
unknown, is in seed (as it were) within
you, as your intelligible character,
pressing to become manifest in
the unique earned character of an
individual life.

THE CALL of a hero on the battlefield, giving his life for his country—this is a hero act equivalent to the Crucifixion. And I think images like this can still activate within you that aspect of your own consciousness and potentialities, which is the noble, the heroic, and the great.

THE INDIVIDUAL must go in quest of his own mythology. His own sanctification, his own justification, his own vivification of his life. It's an individual quest. The institution can help by giving you a few clues, but you've got to do the journey yourself.

EACH OF US has to find his own way. Nobody can give you a mythology. The images that mean something to you, you'll find in your dreams, in your visions, in your actions—and you'll find out what they are after you've passed them. No one in the world was ever you before, with your particular gifts and abilities and possibilities. It's a shame to waste those by doing what someone else has done.

IF YOU'RE FOLLOWING someone else's adventure—if you say, "Oh well, they're wearing things this way this year, so I'm doing that"—that's not your adventure. And you're a fake. And you're going to fall off the bicycle. The adventure has to be yours, really something that has come out of you. And then you can't go wrong. You're in the realm that no one has ever been in before.

NO WAY OR PATH! Because where there is a way or path, it is someone else's path. And that is what marks the Western spirit distinctly from the Eastern. Oriental gurus accept responsibility for their disciples' lives. They have an interesting term, "delegated free will." The guru tells you where you are on the path, who you are, what to do now, and what to do next. The romantic quality of the West, on the other hand, derives from an unprecedented yearning, a yearning for something that has never yet been seen in this world. What can it be that has never yet been seen? What has never yet been seen is your own unprecedented life fulfilled. Your life is what has yet to be brought into being.

NOW THIS BRINGS in a terrific emphasis on what the tender-minded call violence. But that's what nature is. And every now and then you see something that opens your mind to this.... Now can you say yea to that? You've got to. You must have *amor fati*, the love of fate. And it takes an awful lot of guts to *really* say yes all the way.

A REFUSAL of a call that has been heard is very bad, because everything in you knows that a required adventure has been refused. That creates a situation of stagnation.

ONCE THE TREASURE has been grabbed, there is no reconciliation with the powers of the underworld— no sacred marriage, father atonement, nor apotheosis—so there is a violent reaction of the whole unconscious system against the act, and the hero must escape. This is a psychotic condition. You have wrenched some knowledge from the deepest abysses of your unknown self, and now the demons have been loosed to wreak their vengeance.

OFFEN IN ACTUAL LIFE, and not infrequently in the myths and popular tales, we encounter the dull case of the call unanswered; for it is always possible to turn the ear to other interests. Refusal of the summons converts the adventure into its negative. Walled in boredom, hard work, or "culture," the subject loses the power of significant affirmative action and becomes a victim to be saved. His flowering world becomes a wasteland of dry stones and his life feels meaningless—even though, like King Minos, he may through titanic effort succeed in building an empire of renown. Whatever house he builds, it will be a house of death: a labyrinth of cyclopean walls to hide from him his Minotaur. All he can do is create new problems for himself and await the gradual approach of his disintegration.

IN A STRICTLY traditional society, the individual is not allowed to follow the impulse of that individual way. The society has put upon the individual what in India is called his dharma, his duty. The quality of the antithetical mask at first seems to be one of temptation following temptation, disobedience and all. But the individual in our society is urged even to follow that temptation. It's the temptation of your lifestyle, and to follow it requires renunciation as well as conflict. Renunciation of the assured values of the assured support, of the society in which you were born. And there comes a crisis of decision at that moment. Are you going to opt for the assured, the well established and security, or are you going to move uniquely along your own path in the forest of adventure?

ALL OF THE GREAT mythologies and much of the mythic storytelling of the world are from the male point of view. When I was writing *The Hero with a Thousand Faces* and wanted to bring female heroes in, I had to go to the fairy tales. These were told by women to children, you know, and you get a different perspective. It was the men who got involved in spinning most of the great myths. The women were too busy; they had too damn much to do to sit around thinking about stories.

ALL LIFE has drudgery to it.... In Zen, however, even while you're washing the dishes, that's a meditation, that's an act of life. It's not a chore.... Sometimes the drudgery itself can become part of the hero deed.
The point is not to get stuck in the drudgery but to use it to free you.

QUESTING HEROES may ride back and forth over the very ground of the Grail without seeing it: and I am told that in Ireland, one may walk around and right past a fairy hill without seeing it. One seems to be walking a straight line, but actually the line is curving past an invisible fairy hill of glass, which is right there, but hidden— like the Hidden Truth.

THE MIDDLE WAY between heaven and hell is entered through the exercise of three virtues, plus a fourth: 1) disengagement from the fury of the passions, 2) fearlessness in the face of death, 3) indifference to the opinion of the world, and 4) compassion. Throughout Arthurian romance, these are the four tests of the heroes.

IF THE HERO … makes his safe and willing return, he may meet with such a blank misunderstanding and disregard from those whom he has come to help that his career will collapse.

AFFIRMATION IS difficult. We always affirm with conditions. I affirm the world on condition that it gets to be the way Santa Claus told me it ought to be. But affirming it the way it is—that's the hard thing, and that is what rituals are about. Ritual is group participation in the most hideous act, which is the act of life—namely, killing and eating another living thing. We do it together, and this is the way life is. The hero is the one who comes to participate in life courageously and decently, in the way of nature, not in the way of personal rancor, disappointment, or revenge.

TYPICALLY, THE HERO of the fairy tale achieves a domestic, microcosmic triumph, and the hero of myth a world-historical, macrocosmic triumph. Whereas the former—the youngest or despised child who becomes the master of extraordinary powers—prevails over his personal oppressors, the latter brings back from his adventure the means for the regeneration of his society as a whole. Tribal or local heroes, such as the emperor Huang Ti, Moses, or the Aztec Tezcatlipoca, commit their boons to a single folk; universal heroes—Mohammed, Jesus, Gautama Buddha—bring a message for the entire world.

THE VIRTUE of heroism must lie, therefore—according to a view of this kind—not in the will to reform, but in the courage to affirm, the nature of the universe.

ORTEGA Y GASSET talks about the environment and the hero in his *Meditations on Don Quixote*. Don Quixote was the last hero of the Middle Ages. He rode out to encounter giants, but instead of giants, his environment produced windmills. Ortega points out that this story takes place about the time that a mechanistic interpretation of the world came in, so that the environment was no longer spiritually responsive to the hero. The hero is today running up against a hard world that is in no way responsive to his spiritual need.

THE EFFECT of the successful adventure of the hero is the unlocking and release again of the flow of life into the body of the world. The miracle of this flow may be represented in physical terms as a circulation of food substance, dynamically as a streaming of energy, or spiritually as a manifestation of grace.

A HINDU TEXT says, "A dangerous path is this, like the edge of a razor." This is a motif that occurs in medieval literature, also. When Lancelot goes to rescue Guinevere from captivity, he has to cross a stream on a sword's edge with his bare hands and feet, a torrent flowing underneath. When you are doing something that is a brand-new adventure, breaking new ground, whether it is something like a technological breakthrough or simply a way of living that is not what the community can help you with, there's always the danger of too much enthusiasm, of neglecting certain mechanical details. Then you fall off. "A dangerous path is this." When you follow the path of your desire and enthusiasm and emotion, keep your mind in control, and don't let it pull you compulsively into disaster.

THE HERALD or announcer of the adventure … is often dark, loathly, or terrifying, judged evil by the world; yet if one could follow, the way would be opened through the walls of day into the dark where the jewels glow. Or the herald is a beast (as in the fairy tale), representative of the repressed instinctual fecundity within ourselves, or again a veiled mysterious figure—the unknown.

THE SO-CALLED RITES of passage, which occupy such a prominent place in the life of a primitive society (ceremonials of birth, naming, puberty, marriage, burial, etc.), are distinguished by formal, and usually very severe, exercises of severance, whereby the mind is radically cut away from the attitudes, attachments, and life patterns of the stage being left behind. Then follows an interval of more or less extended retirement, during which are enacted rituals designed to introduce the life adventurer to the forms and proper feelings of his new estate, so that when, at last, the time has ripened for the return to the normal world, the initiate will be as good as reborn.

THE GUIDE WITHIN will be his own noble heart alone, and the guide without, the image of beauty, the radiance of divinity, that wakes in his heart *amor*: the deepest, inmost seed of his nature, consubstantial with the process of the All, "thus come." And in this life-creative adventure the criterion of achievement will be, as in every one of the tales here reviewed, the courage to let go the past, with its truths, its goals, its dogmas of "meaning," and its gifts: to die to the world and to come to birth from within.

IN WOLFRAM von Eschenbach's *Parzival*, when Parzival seeks the Grail Castle, he lets the reins lie on the neck of the horse. He could not have guided the horse to the castle; the horse knew where it was and automatically led the way. You have to be guided by nature, not by this head up at the top.

IF THE HERO, instead of submitting to all of the initiatory tests, has, like Prometheus, simply darted to his goal (by violence, quick device, or luck) and plucked the boon for the world that he intended, then the powers that he has unbalanced may react so sharply that he will be blasted from within and without—crucified, like Prometheus, on the rock of his own violated unconscious.

YOU CAN NEVER become your own master until you find your own truth.

IF YOU SAY NO to any detail of your life, you've said no to the whole web because everything is so interlocked. And if you want to get in the way of affirmation, just say no to the failure, the thing that is your most acute shame.

THE USUAL PERSON is more than content, he is even proud, to remain within the indicated bounds, and popular belief gives him every reason to fear so much as the first step into the unexplored.

YOU GET IT time after time in the myths ... the deceptive guide, the one who leads you into the abyss. So you have to be careful; we have plenty of deceptive gurus now—I see them all over the place, and they have very big followings.

THE VISION and the visionary, though apparently separate, are one; and all the heavens, all the hells, all the gods and demons, all the figures of the mythic worlds, are within us as portions of ourselves—portions, that is to say, that are of our deepest, primary nature, and thus of our share in nature. They are out there as well as in here, yet, in this field of consciousness, without separation. Our personal dreams are our personal guides, therefore, to the ranges of myth and of the gods. Dreams are our personal myths; myths, the general dream.

THE HERO, whether god or goddess, man or woman, the figure in a myth or the dreamer of a dream, discovers and assimilates his opposite (his own unsuspected self) either by swallowing it or by being swallowed. One by one the resistances are broken. He must put aside his pride, his virtue, beauty, and life, and bow or submit to the absolutely intolerable. Then he finds that he and his opposite are not of differing species, but one flesh.

THE GOAL of all meditation and mystery journeys is to go between the pair of opposites.

THE AGONY of breaking through personal limitations is the agony of spiritual growth. Art, literature, myth and cult, philosophy, and ascetic disciplines are instruments to help the individual past his limiting horizons into spheres of ever-expanding realization. As he crosses threshold after threshold, conquering dragon after dragon, the stature of the divinity that he summons to his highest wish increases, until it subsumes the cosmos. Finally, the mind breaks the bounding sphere of the cosmos to a realization transcending all experiences of form—all symbolizations, all divinities: a realization of the ineluctable void.

THE JAPANESE have a proverb: "The gods only laugh when men pray to them for wealth." The boon bestowed on the worshipper is always scaled to his stature and to the nature of his dominant desire: the boon is simply a symbol of life energy stepped down to the requirements of a certain specific case. The irony, of course, lies in the fact that, whereas the hero who has won the favor of the god may beg for the boon of perfect illumination, what he generally seeks are longer years to live, weapons with which to slay his neighbor, or the health of his child.

ONCE WE have broken free of the prejudices of our own provincially limited ecclesiastical, tribal, or national rendition of the world archetypes, it becomes possible to understand that the supreme initiation is not that of the local motherly fathers, who then project aggression onto the neighbors for their own defense. The good news, which the World Redeemer brings and which so many have been glad to hear, zealous to preach, but reluctant, apparently, to demonstrate, is that God is love, that He can be, and is to be, loved, and that all without exception are his children.

IN THE OFFICE of the modern psychoanalyst, the stages of the hero-adventure come to light again in the dreams and hallucinations of the patient. Depth beyond depth of self-ignorance is fathomed, with the analyst in the role of the helper, the initiatory priest. And always, after the first thrills of getting under way, the adventure develops into a journey of darkness, horror, disgust, and phantasmagoric fears.

PROTECTIVE POWER is always and ever present within the sanctuary of the heart and even immanent within, or just behind, the unfamiliar features of the world. One has only to know and trust, and the ageless guardians will appear.

IN THE ASCENT of the *kundalini* serpent up the spine—which is another hero journey, note—the final obstacle to overcome, at the transit from the sixth chakra to the seventh, is the barrier between the self and its beloved, the Lord of the Universe—the god that is the world and transcends the world.

THE FIRST STEP, detachment or withdrawal, consists in a radical transfer of emphasis from the external to the internal world, macro- to microcosm, a retreat from the desperations of the wasteland to the peace of the everlasting realm that is within. But this realm, as we know from psychoanalysis, is precisely the infantile unconscious. It is the realm that we enter in sleep. We carry it within ourselves forever. All the ogres and secret helpers of our nursery are there, all the magic of childhood. And more important, all the life-potentialities that we never managed to bring to adult realization, those other portions of ourself, are there; for

such golden seeds do not die. If only
a portion of that lost totality could
be dredged up into the light of day,
we should experience a marvelous
expansion of our powers, a vivid
renewal of life. We should tower in
stature.

THERE ARE (and, apparently, there have always been) two orders of mythology, that of the Village and that of the Forest of Adventure. The imposing guardians of the village rites are those cherubim of the garden gate, their Lordships Fear and Desire, with however another to support them, the Lord Duty, and a fourth, her holiness, Faith: and the aims of their fashionable cults are mainly health, abundance of progeny, long life, wealth, victories in war, and the grace of a painless death. The ways of the Forest Adventurous, on the other hand, are not entered until these guardians have been passed; and the way to pass them is to recognize their apparent power as a figment merely of the restricted field of one's own ego-centered consciousness: not confronting them as "realities" without (for when slain "out there," their power only passes to another vehicle), but shifting the center of one's own horizon of concern. As Joyce's hero, tapping his brow, muses in *Ulysses*: "In here it is I must kill the priest and the king."

PLAYFUL AND unpretentious as the archetypes of fairy tale may appear to be, they are the heroes and villains who have built the world for us. The debutante combing her hair before the glass, the mother pondering the future of a son, the laborer in the mines, the merchant vessel full of cargo, the ambassador with portfolio, the soldier in the field of war—all are working in order that the ungainsayable specifications of effective fantasy, the permanent patterns of the tale of wonder, shall be clothed in flesh and known as life.

THE STORY OF Rip van Winkle is an example of the delicate case of the returning hero. Rip moved into the adventurous realm unconsciously, as we all do every night when we go to sleep. In deep sleep, declare the Hindus, the self is unified and blissful; therefore deep sleep is called the cognitional state. But though we are refreshed and sustained by these nightly visits to the source-darkness, our lives are not reformed by them; we return, like Rip, with nothing to show for the experience but our whiskers.

UNLESS THE MYTHS can be understood—or felt—to be true in some such way as this, they lose their force, their magic, their charm for the tender-minded and become mere archaeological curiosities, fit only for some sort of reductive classification. And this, indeed, would appear to be the death that the heroes of the myths themselves most fear. Continually, they are pointing past and through their phenomenal to their universal, transcendental, aspect. "I and the Father are One," declares the Christ, for example (John 10:30). And Krishna, in the Bhagavad Gita, shows that all the forms of the world are rooted in his metaphysical essence, just as that essence itself, reciprocally, is rooted in all things.

THE AMERICAN workplace is based upon the myth of money. Money is the bottom line today. No value can supersede the value of money. If you want to explain anything that you're doing, turning out third-rate material or anything else, it's cost. You can't turn out what you'd like to turn out because it would cost you too much. The hero is the one who will do it even sacrificing the money. The value that you stand for is your life. And if money is the final term, that's your mythology.

HOW, in the contemporary period, can we evoke the imagery that communicates the most profound and most richly developed sense of experiencing life? These images must point past themselves to that ultimate truth which must be told: that life does not have any one absolutely fixed meaning. These images must point past all meanings given, beyond all definitions and relationships, to that really ineffable mystery that is just the existence, the being of ourselves and of our world. If we give that mystery an exact meaning we diminish the experience of its real depth. But when a poet carries the mind into a context of meanings and then pitches it past those, one knows that marvelous rapture that comes from going past all categories of definition. Here we sense the function of metaphor that allows us to make a journey we could not otherwise make, past all categories of definition.

FOR THE mythological hero is the champion not of things become but of things becoming; the dragon to be slain by him is precisely the monster of the status quo: Holdfast, the keeper of the past. From obscurity the hero emerges, but the enemy is great and conspicuous in the seat of power; he is enemy, dragon, tyrant, because he turns to his own advantage the authority of his position. He is Holdfast not because he keeps the *past* but because he *keeps*.

THE HERO of yesterday becomes the tyrant of tomorrow, unless he crucifies *himself* today.

OUR LIFE evokes our character. You find out more about yourself as you go on. That's why it's good to be able to put yourself in situations that will evoke your higher nature rather than your lower. "Lead us not into temptation."

ARTISTS ARE magical helpers. Evoking symbols and motifs that connect us to our deeper selves, they can help us along the heroic journey of our own lives.

[HEROES HAVE] moved out of the society that would have protected them, and into the dark forest, into the world of fire, of original experience. Original experience has not been interpreted for you, and so you've got to work out your life for yourself. Either you can take it or you can't. You don't have to go far off the interpreted path to find yourself in very difficult situations. The courage to face the trials and to bring a whole new body of possibilities into the field of interpreted experience for other people to experience—that is the hero's deed.

YOU GO INTO the abyss, and you come out. One can go crazy—or one can go through craziness and come out the other side.... The Freudian psychoanalysts generally try to abort the psychosis, knock it out, which can prevent one from going through the whole path, the whole trip, and coming out the other side.

EASTER AND PASSOVER offer the perfect symbols because they mean that we are called to a new life. This new life is not very well defined: that is why we want to hold on to the past. The journey to this new life—and it is a journey we must all make—cannot be made unless we let go of the past. The reality of living in space means that we are born anew, not born again to an old-time religion but to a new order of things. There are no horizons— that is the meaning of the Space Age. We are in a free fall into a future that is mysterious. It is very fluid and this is disconcerting to many people. All you have to do is know how to use a parachute.

A QUESTIONNAIRE was once sent around one of the high schools in Brooklyn which asked, "What would you like to be?" Two-thirds of the students responded, "A celebrity." They had no notion of having to give of themselves in order to achieve something.

WHEN PEOPLE ASK, "Do you believe in reincarnation," I just have to say, "Reincarnation, like heaven, is a metaphor." The metaphor in Christianity that corresponds to reincarnation is purgatory. If one dies with such a fixation on the things of this world that one's spirit is not ready to behold the beatific vision, then one has to undergo a purgation, one has to be purged clean of one's limitations. The limitations are what are called sins. Sin is simply a limiting factor that limits your consciousness and fixes it in an inappropriate condition. In the Oriental metaphor, if you die in that condition, you come back again to have more experiences that will clarify, clarify, clarify, until you are released from these fixations. The reincarnating monad is the principal hero of Oriental myth. The monad puts on various personalities, life after life. Now the reincarnation idea is not that you and I as the personalities that we are will be reincarnated. The personality is what the monad throws off. Then the monad puts on another body, male or female, depending on what experiences are necessary for it to clear itself of this attachment to the field of time.

[THE] SCIENTIFIC method was itself a product of the minds of already self-reliant individuals courageous enough to be free. Moreover, not only in the sciences but in every department of life the will and courage to credit one's own senses and to honor one's own decisions, to name one's own virtues, and to claim one's own vision of truth, have been the generative forces of the new age, the enzymes of the fermentation of the wine of this great modern harvest—which is a wine, however, that can be safely drunk only by those with a courage of their own.

IF YOU REALIZE what the real problem is—losing yourself, giving yourself to some higher end, or to another—you realize that this itself is the ultimate trial. When we quit thinking primarily about ourselves and our own self-preservation, we undergo a truly heroic transformation of consciousness. And what all the myths have to deal with is transformations of consciousness of one kind or another. You have been thinking one way, you now have to think a different way.

THE HERO is the man of self-achieved submission. But submission to what? That precisely is the riddle that today we have to ask ourselves and that it is everywhere the primary virtue and historic deed of the hero to have solved.... Within the soul, within the body social, there must be—if we are to experience long survival—a continuous "recurrence of birth" (*palingenesia*) to nullify the unremitting recurrences of death. For it is by means of our own victories, if we are not regenerated, that the work of Nemesis is wrought: doom breaks from the shell of our very virtue. Peace then is a snare; war is a snare; change is a snare; permanence a snare. When

our day is come for the victory of
death, death closes in; there is nothing
we can do, except be crucified—and
resurrected; dismembered totally, and
then reborn.

THE FIRST GOAL of any shining hero seeking to release the values of the spirit from the guardianship of such unimaginative worms must be to lance them, like a knight, and break the hold of their dragon grip. Accordingly the yogi, by deep and measured breathing, appropriate meditations, controlled body postures, hand postures, the recitation of stirring syllables, and so on, will strive to wake the torpid serpent of his spiritual life from its lethargy, its sleep, its unadventurous dream, to better things; lifting it, in its full, unfolding length, up the long spinal course to the crown, and rousing on its way all the other lotuses of our human potential to their flowering.

THE LAST ACT in the biography of the hero is that of the death or departure. Here the whole sense of the life is epitomized. Needless to say, the hero would be no hero if death held for him any terror; the first condition is reconciliation with the grave.

THEN COMES the real problem of return to the world you had left with what you have found—and the introduction of that to the world you've left, so that there's a harmonious environment in accord with the requirements of your own nature. You don't have a complete adventure unless you do get back. There's a time to go out in the woods, and there's a time to come back. And you *know* which it is, you really do. That's a bit dicey, a major problem not only in the spiritual life, but in any kind of questing and finding. Do you have the courage? It takes a hell of a lot of courage to come back after you've been in the woods.

THE SECRET CAUSE of your death is your destiny. Every life has a limitation, and in challenging the limit you are bringing the limit closer to you, and the heroes are the ones who initiate their actions no matter what destiny may result. What happens is, therefore, a function of what the person does. This is true of life all the way through. Here is revealed the secret cause: your own life course is the secret cause of your death.

IT'S A WONDERFUL thing having been thrown out with no job, hunting my own way. I found things that other people were going to need when they lost their way too. The saying a friend of mine has given me for letting me know when you are in late middle age is: you've got to the top of the ladder and found it's against the wrong wall. Well, I think I found what it is you need to break through that wall. This is one of the delights of my experience.

I DON'T THINK there is any such thing as an ordinary mortal. Everybody has his own possibility of rapture in the experience of life. All he has to do is recognize it and then cultivate it and get going with it. I always feel uncomfortable when people speak about ordinary mortals because I've never met an ordinary man, woman, or child.

TODAY THE WALLS and towers of the culture-world that [in centuries past] were in the building are dissolving; and whereas heroes then could set forth of their own will from the known to the unknown, we today, willy-nilly, must enter the forest *la ou nos la voions plus espesse* [where we see it to be thickest]: and, like it or not, the pathless way is the only way now before us.

THE CONQUEST of the fear of death is the recovery of life's joy. One can experience an unconditional affirmation of life only when one has accepted death, not as contrary to life but as an aspect of life. Life in its becoming is always shedding death, and on the point of death. The conquest of fear yields the courage of life. That is the cardinal initiation of every heroic adventure—fearlessness and achievement.

THE MODERN HERO, the modern individual who dares to heed the call and seek the mansion of that presence with whom it is our whole destiny to be atoned, cannot, indeed must not, wait for his community to cast off its slough of pride, fear, rationalized avarice, and sanctified misunderstanding. "Live," Nietzsche says, "as though the day were here." It is not society that is to guide and save the creative hero, but precisely the reverse. And so every one of us shares the supreme ordeal—carries the cross of the redeemer—not in the bright moments of his tribe's great victories, but in the silences of his personal despair.

THE BIG MOMENT in the medieval myth is the awakening of the heart to compassion, the transformation of passion into compassion. That is the whole problem of the Grail stories, compassion for the wounded king. And out of that you also get the notion that Abelard offered as an explanation of the crucifixion: that the Son of God came down into this world to be crucified to awaken our hearts to compassion, and thus to turn our minds from the gross concerns of raw life in the world to the specifically human values of self-giving in shared suffering. In that sense the wounded king, the maimed king of the Grail legend, is a counterpart of the Christ.

HE IS THERE to evoke compassion and thus bring a dead wasteland to life. There is a mystical notion there of the spiritual function of suffering in this world. The one who suffers is, as it were, the Christ, come before us to evoke the one thing that turns the human beast of prey into a valid human being. That one thing is compassion. This is the theme that James Joyce takes over and develops in *Ulysses*—the awakening of his hero, Stephen Dedalus, to manhood through a shared compassion with Leopold Bloom. That was the awakening of his heart to love and the opening of the way.

THE ILLUMINATION is the recognition of the radiance of one eternity through all things, whether in the vision of time these things are judged as good or as evil. To come to this, you must release yourself completely from desiring the goods of this world and fearing their loss. "Judge not that you be not judged," we read in the words of Jesus. "If the doors of perception were cleansed," wrote Blake, "man would see everything as it is, infinite."

IT'S IMPORTANT to live life with the experience, and therefore the knowledge, of its mystery and of your own mystery. This gives life a new radiance, a new harmony, a new splendor. Thinking in mythological terms helps to put you in accord with the inevitables of this vale of tears. You learn to recognize the positive values in what appear to be the negative moments and aspects of your life. The big question is whether you are going to be able to say a hearty yes to your adventure . . . the adventure of the hero—the adventure of being alive.

THE CHALLENGE of the moment—and there are many who are meeting it, accepting it, and responding to it, in the way not of men but of women—the challenge is to flower as individuals, neither as biological archetypes nor as personalities imitative of the male. And, to repeat, there are no models in our mythology for an individual woman's quest. Nor is there any model for the male in marriage to an individuated female. We are in this thing together and have to work it out together, not with passion (which is always archetypal) but with *compassion*, in patient fostering of each other's growth.

WE HAVE NOT even to risk the adventure alone; for the heroes of all time have gone before us; the labyrinth is thoroughly known; we have only to follow the thread of the hero-path. And where we had thought to find an abomination, we shall find a god; where we had thought to slay another, we shall slay ourselves; where we had thought to travel outward, we shall come to the center of our own existence; where we had thought to be alone, we shall be with all the world.

SOURCE TEXTS

Correspondence: 1927–1987

Flight of the Wild Gander: Explorations in the Mythical Dimension

Goddesses: Mysteries of the Feminine Divine

The Hero with a Thousand Faces

The Hero's Journey: Joseph Campbell on His Life and Work

"Jungian Psychology: Jung Myth & Shadow" (lecture)

The Masks of God, Volume 2: Oriental Mythology

The Masks of God, Volume 3: Occidental Mythology

The Masks of God, Volume 4: Creative Mythology

Myth and Meaning: Conversations on Mythology and Life

The Mythic Dimension: Selected Essays 1959–1987

Pathways to Bliss: Mythology and Personal Transformation

The Power of Myth

"Psychosis and the Hero's Journey" (lecture)

Romance of the Grail: The Magic and Mystery of Arthurian Myth

Thou Art That: Transforming Religious Metaphor

ABOUT JOSEPH CAMPBELL

Joseph Campbell (1904–1987) was a renowned American author and scholar of comparative mythology. His groundbreaking work *The Hero with a Thousand Faces* (1949) introduced the concept of the "hero's journey," a universal pattern found in myths across cultures. Campbell's theories were influenced by his studies in Europe, the work of Picasso and Joyce, Freud's and Jung's theories about the human psyche, his lifelong interest in Native American cultures, and his translation with Swami Nikhilananda of the Upanishads and *The Gospel of Sri Ramakrishna*. In 1988, the PBS series *The Power of Myth* brought his ideas to a global audience, solidifying his legacy in the study of mythology.

THE JOSEPH CAMPBELL FOUNDATION
(JCF) is a not-for-profit corporation that continues the work of Joseph Campbell, exploring the fields of mythology and comparative religion. The Foundation is guided by three principal goals: First, the Joseph Campbell Foundation preserves, protects, and perpetuates Campbell's pioneering work. Second, the Foundation promotes the study of mythology and comparative religion. Third, the Foundation helps individuals enrich their lives by experiencing the power of myth through community outreach and periodic Joseph Campbell–related events and activities.

JCF.org
John Bucher, Executive Director
Bradley Olson, Director of Publications